BECOME SELF-MOTIVATED

Tips and Strategies for Achieving Success and Happiness

TABLE OF CONTENTS

INTRODUCTION

DEFINITION OF SELF-MOTIVATION

The ability to initiate and sustain effort toward achieving a goal or making progress without the need for external encouragement or rewards is referred to as self-motivation. It is an internal desire to accomplish something, and it can be a powerful force that helps us overcome obstacles and setbacks. Self-motivation can be influenced by a variety of factors, including personal values, goals, and interests, and it can help us stay focused and committed to our goals even when we face obstacles or setbacks. Individuals who are self-motivated can take ownership of their actions and work with determination and persistence toward their goals. Overall, self-motivation is a necessary component of personal development and success.

THE IMPORTANCE OF SELF-MOTIVATION IN ACHIEVING SUCCESS AND HAPPINESS

Self-motivation is a necessary trait that can assist us in achieving success in many areas of our lives, including our careers, personal relationships, and personal development. We are more likely to initiate and sustain effort toward our goals when we are self-motivated, which can lead to increased productivity and achievement. Furthermore, self-motivation can help us overcome obstacles and setbacks by allowing us to persevere and stay focused even when faced with difficulties.

Self-motivation can also play an important role in happiness. We are more likely to feel a sense of accomplishment and satisfaction when we are motivated to pursue our goals and interests, which can contribute to our overall happiness and well-being. Furthermore, self-motivation can make us feel more in control of our lives and provide us with a sense of purpose and direction.

Overall, self-motivation is an important factor in achieving success and happiness because it allows us to initiate and sustain effort toward our goals, overcome challenges, and feel a sense of accomplishment and satisfaction.

UNDERSTANDING YOUR GOALS AND VALUES

IDENTIFYING YOUR GOALS AND VALUES

Identifying your goals and values is a critical step in the self-motivation process. Goals are specific objectives or targets that you wish to achieve, whereas values are guiding principles or beliefs that influence your actions and decisions. You can better understand what motivates you and what is most important to you if you understand your goals and values.

Begin by asking yourself some questions to help you identify your goals and values, such as:

What do I want to achieve in life?

What are my long-term and short-term goals?

What are my passions and interests?

What are the most important things to me in life?

What do I stand for and believe in?

Answering these questions can help you better understand your goals and values. It may also be beneficial to write down your responses or discuss them with someone.

After you've identified your values and goals, you can prioritize them and set specific, measurable, achievable, relevant, and time-bound (SMART) goals. This can help you focus on what is most important and create a plan for achieving your objectives. Setting SMART goals entails defining your objectives in a specific and measurable manner, making them achievable and realistic, ensuring that they are relevant to your overall goals and values, and establishing a timetable for achieving them. This can assist you in staying motivated and on track as you work toward your objectives.

Identifying your goals and values is an important step in the self-motivation process because it allows you to understand what is most important to you and set specific and attainable goals.

SETTING SPECIFIC, MEASURABLE, ACHIEVABLE, RELEVANT, AND TIME-BOUND (SMART) GOALS

Setting SMART goals is a popular method for establishing and achieving specific, attainable goals. SMART goals are specific, measurable, achievable, relevant, and time-bound objectives that can help you stay motivated and on track as you work toward your goals.

Specific:

Your goals should be specific and clearly defined, rather than vague or general. For example, instead of setting a goal to "exercise more," you might set a goal to "exercise for 30 minutes three times per week."

Measurable:

Your goals should be measurable, so that you can track your progress and determine whether you have achieved them. For example, you might set a goal to "lose 10 pounds" or to "save $500 in the next six months."

Achievable:

Your goals should be achievable and realistic, given your current resources and circumstances. It's important to stretch yourself but setting unrealistic goals can lead to frustration and disappointment.

Relevant:

Your goals should be relevant and aligned with your overall goals and values. This can help you to stay motivated and focused on what is most important to you.

Time-bound:

Your goals should have a specific timeline, so that you can stay on track and stay motivated. This might be a specific date, or it might be a specific period of time.

By setting SMART goals, you can increase your chances of achieving your objectives and staying motivated as you work towards them. It's important to review your progress regularly and to adjust as needed to ensure that you are on track to achieve your goals.

THE ROLE OF VALUES IN MOTIVATING YOURSELF

Values are the guiding principles or beliefs that guide your actions and decisions, and they can be very motivating. You can increase your motivation and drive to achieve your goals by understanding your values and aligning your actions with them.

You can identify your values by asking yourself questions like:

What are the most important aspects of my life?

What do I stand for and what do I believe in?

What characteristics or qualities are important to me?

Answering these questions can help you to gain a clearer understanding of your values. You may also find it helpful to write down your responses or to talk to someone about them.

Once you have identified your values, you can use them to motivate yourself in several ways. For example:

Set goals that align with your values:

By setting goals that are aligned with your values, you can increase your motivation and commitment to achieving them.

For example, if one of your values is health, you might set a goal to start exercising regularly.

Use your values as a source of inspiration:

Your values can serve as a source of inspiration and motivation when you are feeling stuck or demotivated. For example, if one of your values is service to others, you might remind yourself of this value when you are feeling uninspired and use it to motivate yourself to act.

Reflect on your values regularly:

Taking time to reflect on your values can help you to stay motivated and focused on what is most important to you. You might find it helpful to write down your values and to review them regularly, or to talk to someone about them.

Overall, understanding and aligning your actions with your values can be a powerful way to motivate yourself and stay focused on your goals.

OVERCOMING OBSTACLES AND SETBACKS

DEALING WITH PROCRASTINATION AND LACK OF MOTIVATION

Procrastination and lack of motivation can be common challenges that can get in the way of achieving our goals. However, there are strategies that you can use to overcome these challenges and stay motivated.

Identify the root cause of your procrastination or lack of motivation:

It can be helpful to identify the underlying cause of your procrastination or lack of motivation. For example, you might be procrastinating because you are feeling overwhelmed or because you are unsure of how to get started on a task. Once you have identified the root cause, you can take steps to address it.

Set specific, achievable goals:

Setting specific, achievable goals can help to increase your motivation and focus. By breaking down your goals into smaller, more manageable tasks, you can feel more in control and more motivated to get started.

Create a positive, distraction-free environment:

Your environment can have a big impact on your motivation and focus. Try to create a positive, distraction-free environment that is conducive to productivity and focus. This might involve removing distractions, such as turning off notifications on your phone, or creating a designated work area.

Find an accountability partner:

Having someone to check in with and hold you accountable can be a helpful way to stay motivated and on track. You might find it helpful to work with a friend or colleague, or to hire a coach or mentor.

Take breaks and reward yourself:

Taking breaks and rewarding yourself can help to keep you motivated and energized. Don't be afraid to take breaks when you need them and celebrate your progress and achievements along the way.

Overall, there are many strategies that you can use to overcome procrastination and lack of motivation and stay focused on your goals. By identifying the root cause, setting specific goals, creating a positive environment, finding accountability, and taking breaks and rewarding yourself, you can stay motivated and make progress towards your goals.

COPING WITH FAILURE AND SETBACKS

Failure and setbacks are an inevitable part of life, and it's important to have strategies in place for coping with them. By learning how to cope with failure and setbacks, you can stay motivated and continue working towards your goals.

Acknowledge your feelings:

It's natural to feel disappointed or frustrated when you experience a failure or setback. It's important to allow yourself to feel these emotions and to acknowledge them, rather than trying to ignore or suppress them.

Reflect on the experience:

Take some time to reflect on the experience of failure or setback. What went well? What could have gone better? What did you learn from the experience? Reflecting on the experience can help you to identify any areas for improvement and to develop strategies for coping with future challenges.

Don't give up:

It can be tempting to give up when you experience a failure or setback, but it's important to remember that these experiences are a normal part of the journey towards success. Instead of giving up, try to reframe your failure or setback as an opportunity to learn and grow.

Seek support:

It can be helpful to seek support from friends, family, or a professional when you are coping with a failure or setback. Having someone to talk to can help you to process your feelings and to find ways to move forward.

Set a new goal:

Set a new goal or create a plan for how you will move forward. This can help you to stay motivated and to refocus your efforts on something positive.

Overall, failure and setbacks are an inevitable part of life, but by acknowledging your feelings, reflecting on the experience, not giving up, seeking support, and setting a new goal, you can stay motivated and continue working towards your goals.

FINDING WAYS TO STAY MOTIVATED WHEN FACED WITH CHALLENGES

There are many strategies that you can use to stay motivated when faced with challenges. By finding ways to maintain your motivation, you can continue working towards your goals and overcome obstacles and setbacks.

Keep your goals in mind: It can be helpful to remind yourself of your goals and the reasons why you are pursuing them. This can help you to stay focused and motivated, even when faced with challenges.

Find ways to stay engaged and interested: Engaging in activities that are meaningful and interesting to you can help to keep you motivated. Find ways to incorporate your passions and interests into your work or goals and try to find joy and fulfillment in the process.

Seek out new challenges and opportunities: Challenges can be a source of motivation, as they provide an opportunity to learn and grow. Seek out new challenges and opportunities to keep yourself motivated and engaged.

Celebrate your progress and accomplishments: It's important to celebrate your progress and accomplishments along the way.

Recognize and appreciate the hard work and effort that you have put in and use these successes as motivation to continue moving forward.

Seek support: Having a support network can be a powerful source of motivation. Surround yourself with positive, supportive people who can help to lift you up and encourage you when you are faced with challenges.

Overall, there are many strategies that you can use to stay motivated when faced with challenges. By keeping your goals in mind, finding ways to stay engaged and interested, seeking out new challenges and opportunities, celebrating your progress and accomplishments, and seeking support, you can maintain your motivation and continue working towards your goals.

BUILDING A POSITIVE MINDSET

THE POWER OF POSITIVE THINKING

Positive thinking is the practice of focusing on the positive aspects of a situation or challenge, rather than dwelling on the negative. It involves actively reframing negative thoughts and adopting a more optimistic and hopeful perspective. Research has shown that positive thinking can have a powerful impact on our well-being and can even affect our physical health.

Increased motivation and productivity:

By adopting a positive mindset, you may find that you are more motivated and productive. When you focus on the positive aspects of a task or challenge, you may be more likely to initiate and sustain effort towards your goals.

Improved well-being:

Positive thinking has been linked to increased feelings of happiness and well-being. When you focus on the positive aspects of your life, you may experience increased satisfaction and enjoyment.

Increased resilience:

Positive thinking can help to increase your resilience and your ability to cope with challenges and setbacks. By focusing on the positive aspects of a situation, you may be more likely to persevere and stay motivated in the face of obstacles.

27

Improved physical health:

Research has shown that positive thinking can have a positive impact on physical health. Positive thinking has been linked to improved immune function, lower blood pressure, and a reduced risk of certain chronic conditions.

Overall, the power of positive thinking can be significant, and it can be a valuable tool for increasing motivation, well-being, resilience, and physical health.

STRATEGIES FOR CULTIVATING A POSITIVE MINDSET

Cultivating a positive mindset involves actively focusing on the positive aspects of a situation or challenge, rather than dwelling on the negative. It involves reframing negative thoughts and adopting a more optimistic and hopeful perspective. Cultivating a positive mindset can be beneficial in terms of increased motivation and productivity, improved well-being, increased resilience, and improved physical health. There are various strategies that you can use to cultivate a positive mindset, such as practicing gratitude, reframing negative thoughts, engaging in positive self-talk, seeking out positive influences, and taking care of yourself.

Practice gratitude:

Focusing on the things that you are grateful for can help to shift your perspective and cultivate a more positive mindset. Try keeping a gratitude journal, in which you write down three things that you are grateful for each day.

Reframe negative thoughts:

When negative thoughts arise, try to reframe them in a more positive light. For example, instead of thinking "I can't do this," try thinking "I may not have done this before, but I am capable of learning and growing."

Engage in positive self-talk:

Pay attention to the words that you use when you talk to yourself, and try to use positive, supportive language. Avoid using negative self-talk, such as "I'm not good enough" or "I'll never be able to do this."

Seek out positive influences:

Surround yourself with people and activities that are positive and uplifting. Avoid negative influences that drain your energy or bring you down.

Take care of yourself:

Self-care is an important aspect of cultivating a positive mindset. Make sure to prioritize self-care activities, such as exercise, rest, and relaxation, in order

THE BENEFITS OF A POSITIVE ATTITUDE

A positive attitude can increase your motivation and productivity, improve your well-being, increase your resilience, improve your relationships with others, and even improve your physical health. A positive attitude allows you to focus on the positive aspects of a situation or challenge, rather than dwelling on the negative, and it can help you to persevere and stay motivated in the face of obstacles. By cultivating a positive attitude, you can increase your chances of success and happiness in life.

Increased motivation and productivity:

A positive attitude can help to increase your motivation and productivity, as it allows you to focus on the positive aspects of a task or challenge rather than dwelling on the negative. When you have a positive attitude, you may be more likely to initiate and sustain effort towards your goals.

Improved well-being:

A positive attitude has been linked to increased feelings of happiness and well-being. When you have a positive outlook on life, you may experience increased satisfaction and enjoyment.

Increased resilience:

A positive attitude can help to increase your resilience and your ability to cope with challenges and setbacks. When you have a positive attitude, you may be more likely to persevere and stay motivated in the face of obstacles.

Improved relationships:

A positive attitude can help to improve your relationships with others. When you have a positive outlook, you may be more likely to form and maintain positive and supportive relationships.

Improved physical health:

Research has shown that a positive attitude can have a positive impact on physical health. A positive attitude has been linked to improved immune function, lower blood pressure, and a reduced risk of certain chronic conditions.

Overall, a positive attitude can have a range of benefits, including increased motivation and productivity, improved well-being, increased resilience, improved relationships, and improved physical health.

DEVELOPING HEALTHY HABITS AND ROUTINES

THE IMPORTANCE OF ESTABLISHING HEALTHY HABITS AND ROUTINES

Establishing healthy habits and routines can be an important part of achieving your goals and leading a fulfilling life. Healthy habits and routines can help you to stay motivated, focused, and productive, and they can contribute to your overall well-being.

Increased productivity and efficiency:

Establishing healthy habits and routines can help you to be more productive and efficient. By creating a routine, you can reduce the amount of time and energy that you spend on tasks, and you can focus on what is most important to you.

Improved health and well-being:

Healthy habits and routines, such as regular exercise and a healthy diet, can contribute to improved physical and mental health. By establishing healthy habits and routines, you can improve your overall well-being and reduce your risk of certain health conditions.

Increased sense of control and accomplishment:

Establishing healthy habits and routines can help you to feel more in control of your life and to accomplish your goals. By setting clear goals and creating a plan to achieve them, you can increase your sense of accomplishment and satisfaction.

Reduced stress and anxiety:

Establishing healthy habits and routines can help to reduce stress and anxiety, as they provide a sense of structure and predictability. By creating routines for tasks such as exercise, sleep, and relaxation, you can better manage your stress and reduce your risk of burnout.

Overall, establishing healthy habits and routines can be an important part of achieving your goals and leading a fulfilling life. By creating routines and developing healthy habits, you can increase your productivity, improve your health and well-being, increase your sense of control and accomplishment, and reduce your stress and anxiety.

TIPS FOR CREATING AND MAINTAINING HEALTHY HABITS AND ROUTINES

Start small:

It can be overwhelming to try to make big changes all at once. Instead, try starting small and building on your successes. For example, if you want to start exercising regularly, try committing to just a few minutes of exercise each day, and gradually increase the amount of time as you become more comfortable.

Make it easy:

Make it as easy as possible to engage in healthy habits and routines. For example, if you want to start exercising regularly, choose an activity that you enjoy and that is convenient for you. You might also consider setting aside a designated time for exercise each day or creating a supportive environment that makes it easier to engage in your chosen activity.

Make it a habit:

Habits are formed when we repeat an action consistently over time. To create a healthy habit, try to engage in the desired behavior consistently, and aim to do so at the same time each day. This can help to turn the behavior into a routine that becomes automatic.

Find accountability:

Having someone to hold you accountable can be a helpful way to stay motivated and on track. You might find it helpful to work with a friend or colleague, or to hire a coach or mentor.

Celebrate your progress and accomplishments:

It's important to celebrate your progress and accomplishments along the way. Recognize and appreciate the hard work and effort that you have put in and use these successes as motivation to continue moving forward.

Overall, creating and maintaining healthy habits and routines requires consistency, effort, and a supportive environment. By starting small, making it easy, turning it into a habit, seeking accountability, and celebrating your progress and accomplishments, you can establish and maintain healthy habits and routines that contribute to your overall well-being and success.

THE ROLE OF DISCIPLINE IN SELF-MOTIVATION

Discipline is the ability to control one's actions, thoughts, and feelings to achieve a goal or maintain a standard of behavior. Discipline is an important aspect of self-motivation, as it allows you to stay focused and committed to your goals, even when faced with challenges or distractions.

Helps you to stay focused and on track:

Discipline helps you to stay focused and on track, even when faced with distractions or challenges. By setting clear goals and maintaining a consistent routine, you can stay motivated and make progress towards your goals.

Increases your sense of accomplishment:

Discipline allows you to follow through on your commitments and to achieve your goals. By setting and achieving goals, you can increase your sense of accomplishment and satisfaction, which can help to boost your motivation.

Builds self-confidence:

Discipline allows you to develop self-confidence and self-esteem, as you learn to rely on yourself and your own abilities to achieve your goals. When you have self-confidence, you may be more likely to take on new challenges and to stay motivated in the face of obstacles.

Enhances your self-control:

Discipline helps to enhance your self-control, which can be an important aspect of self-motivation. By developing self-control, you can better manage your thoughts, feelings, and actions, and you can stay focused on your goals.

Overall, discipline is an important aspect of self-motivation, as it helps you to stay focused and on track, increases your sense of accomplishment, builds self-confidence, and enhances your self-control. By cultivating discipline, you can increase your chances of achieving your goals and leading a fulfilling life.

SEEKING SUPPORT AND ACCOUNTABILITY

THE VALUE OF HAVING A SUPPORT SYSTEM

Having a support system can be an important aspect of self-motivation, as it provides a network of people who can offer encouragement, guidance, and motivation when you need it. A support system can consist of friends, family, colleagues, mentors, or professionals, and it can provide a sense of connection and belonging.

Encouragement and motivation:

A support system can provide encouragement and motivation when you need it. When you are facing challenges or setbacks, it can be helpful to have someone to talk to and to offer support.

Guidance and advice:

A support system can provide guidance and advice when you are faced with decisions or challenges. By seeking input from others, you can gain valuable perspective and insights that can help you to stay motivated and on track.

A sense of connection and belonging:

A support system provides a sense of connection and belonging, which can be an important aspect of self-motivation. When you feel connected to others and part of a community, you may be more likely to stay motivated and engaged.

A source of accountability:

A support system can provide accountability, which can be a helpful way to stay motivated and on track. By sharing your goals and progress with others, you can receive feedback and encouragement, and you can stay accountable to yourself and your commitments.

Overall, having a support system can be an important aspect of self-motivation, as it provides encouragement, guidance, a sense of connection and belonging, and a source of accountability. By cultivating a support system, you can increase your chances of success and happiness.

FINDING AND BUILDING A SUPPORT NETWORK

Identify your needs:

Before you can start building a support network, it can be helpful to identify your needs and what type of support you are looking for. Are you seeking encouragement, guidance, accountability, or something else? By identifying your needs, you can better determine what type of support you are looking for and who might be able to provide it.

Look for people who share your values and goals:

It can be helpful to seek out people who share your values and goals, as they may be more likely to understand and support your efforts. Look for people who are interested in similar things or who have similar goals and consider joining groups or organizations that align with your interests.

Reach out to others:

Don't be afraid to reach out to others and ask for support. This can be intimidating, but it can also be a powerful way to build relationships and to find the support that you need. Consider reaching out to friends, family, colleagues, or professionals who you think might be able to help.

Be open and authentic:

When building a support network, it's important to be open and authentic. Share your goals and challenges and be willing to ask for help when you need it. By being genuine and open, you can build strong and supportive relationships.

Foster and maintain relationships:

Building a support network requires effort and commitment. Try to foster and maintain your relationships and be there for others when they need support. This can help to build a strong and supportive network over time.

Overall, building a support network requires identifying your needs, seeking out people who share your values and goals, reaching out to others, being open and authentic, and fostering and maintaining relationships. By building a support network, you can gain access to valuable encouragement, guidance, and accountability that can help you to stay motivated and on track.

THE ROLE OF ACCOUNTABILITY IN SELF-MOTIVATION

Accountability refers to the obligation to answer to someone or something for your actions, decisions, or performance. Accountability is an important aspect of self-motivation, as it can help you to stay on track and to follow through on your commitments.

Here are a few ways in which accountability can contribute to self-motivation:

Increases your sense of commitment:

When you are accountable to someone else, you may feel more committed to your goals and more motivated to follow through on your commitments. By sharing your goals with others and seeking accountability, you can increase your sense of commitment and your chances of success.

Provides a source of motivation:

Being accountable to someone else can provide a source of motivation and encouragement. When you have someone to report to, you may feel more motivated to stay on track and to achieve your goals.

Increases your focus:

Accountability can help to increase your focus and to stay on track, as you are responsible for meeting certain expectations or standards. By setting clear goals and seeking accountability, you can stay focused and motivated to achieve your goals.

Enhances your self-control:

Accountability can help to enhance your self-control, as you are responsible for your actions and decisions. By seeking accountability, you can better manage your thoughts, feelings, and actions, and you can stay motivated and on track.

Overall, accountability is an important aspect of self-motivation, as it increases your sense of commitment, provides a source of motivation, increases your focus, and enhances your self-control. By seeking accountability, you can increase your chances of achieving your goals and leading a fulfilling life.

CONCLUSION

RECAP OF KEY POINTS

Self-motivation refers to the ability to initiate and sustain effort towards a goal, and it is an important aspect of achieving success and happiness.

Identifying your goals and values is an important step in self-motivation, as it helps you to clarify what is most important to you and to set clear and meaningful goals.

Setting specific, measurable, achievable, relevant, and time-bound (SMART) goals can help you to stay motivated and on track, as it provides a clear and actionable plan for achieving your goals.

The role of values in motivating yourself is important, as they provide a sense of purpose and meaning. By aligning your goals with your values, you can increase your motivation and sense of fulfillment.

Dealing with procrastination and lack of motivation can be challenging, but there are strategies that you can use to overcome these obstacles. These strategies include setting clear goals, breaking tasks down into smaller steps, and seeking accountability.

Coping with failure and setbacks is an important aspect of self-motivation, as it allows you to learn from your mistakes and to stay motivated and on track. Strategies for coping with failure and setbacks include reframing negative thoughts, learning from mistakes, and seeking support.

Finding ways to stay motivated when faced with challenges is an important aspect of self-motivation. Strategies for staying motivated when faced with challenges include setting clear goals, seeking support, practicing gratitude, and engaging in positive self-talk.

The power of positive thinking is an important aspect of self-motivation, as it allows you to focus on the positive aspects of a situation and to stay motivated and on track. Strategies for cultivating a positive mindset include practicing gratitude, reframing negative thoughts, engaging in positive self-talk, seeking out positive influences, and taking care of yourself.

Establishing healthy habits and routines can be an important part of self-motivation, as it helps you to stay focused

ACT AND START YOUR JOURNEY TOWARDS SELF-MOTIVATION

If you want to achieve your goals and lead a fulfilling life, it is important to act and become self-motivated. While it can be easy to get stuck in a rut or to feel overwhelmed by challenges, it is important to remember that motivation is not something that you either have or don't have - it is something that you can cultivate and develop. With the right tools and strategies, you can learn to become self-motivated and to act towards your goals.

Identify your goals and values:

To become self-motivated, it is important to clarify what is most important to you and to set clear and meaningful goals. By identifying your goals and values, you can gain a sense of purpose and direction, which can help to increase your motivation.

Set SMART goals:

Setting specific, measurable, achievable, relevant, and time-bound (SMART) goals can help you to stay motivated and on track. SMART goals provide a clear and actionable plan for achieving your goals, and they can help you to stay focused and motivated.

Break tasks down into smaller steps:

If you are feeling overwhelmed or unsure where to start, it can be helpful to break tasks down into smaller steps. By taking things one step at a time, you can build momentum and stay motivated.

Seek accountability:

Seeking accountability can be a helpful way to stay motivated and on track. By sharing your goals with others and seeking accountability, you can increase your sense of commitment and your chances of success.

Take small, consistent steps:

Taking small, consistent steps towards your goals can be an important aspect of self-motivation, as it helps you to build momentum and to stay motivated. When you act, even if it is just a little bit at a time, you can begin to make progress and to see the results of your efforts. This can be a powerful way to stay motivated and to continue moving forward.

Disclosure:

This book was written with the help of AI software. While the ideas and concepts presented in this book are based on research and the experience of the author, the actual writing and organization of the content was assisted by AI software. The goal of this software was to help the author to convey the ideas and concepts of the book more efficiently and effectively, and to assist with the overall structure and organization of the content. The author has reviewed and edited the content to ensure accuracy and clarity, and to ensure that it aligns with the overall goals and themes of the book.